From Beans to Chocolate Bars

Carmel Reilly

From Beans to Chocolate Bars

Text: Carmel Reilly
Publishers: Tania Mazzeo and Eliza Webb
Series consultant: Amanda Sutera
 Hands on Heads Consulting
Editor: Jarrah Moore
Project editor: Annabel Smith
Designer: Leigh Ashforth
Project designer: Danielle Maccarone
Illustrations: Sara Lynn Cramb
Permissions researcher: Debbie Gallagher
Production controller: Renee Tome

Acknowledgements
We would like to thank the following for permission to reproduce copyright material:

Font cover: Shutterstock.com/stockcreations; pp. 1, 7; iStock.com/Inna Tarasenko; pp. 3, 4 (left), back cover (bottom): iStock.com/kjohansen; p. 4 (right), back cover (top): iStock.com/barbaraaaa; p. 5 (bottom): Shutterstock.com/Aleksandr Rybalko; p. 6 (main): Shutterstock.com/Clark Ahlstrom, (inset): Shutterstock.com/tristan tan; p. 8 (top): Shutterstock.com/CKP1001, (bottom): Alamy Stock Photo/Greenshoots Communications; p. 9 (top): Getty Images/Jan Sochor, (bottom): Getty Images/David Ryder/Bloomberg; p. 10 (top): Alamy Stock Photo/Mariusz Szczawinski, (bottom): iStock.com/Floortje; p. 11 (top): iStock.com/Michel VIARD, (bottom): Shutterstock.com/AmyLv; p. 12: iStock.com/deyangeorgiev; p. 13 (top): iStock.com/Oksana Kuznetsova, (bottom): Alamy Stock Photo/Mark Fagelson; p. 14: Shutterstock.com/bigacis; p. 16 (top): iStock.com/LisaStrachan, (bottom): Getty Images/Monty Rakusen; pp. 17 (top), 23: iStock.com/subjug; p. 17 (bottom): iStock.com/xavierarnau; p. 18: Alamy Stock Photo/Takatoshi Kurikawa; p. 19: iStock.com/HelpingHandPhotos; p. 20 (top): iStock.com/xavierarnau, (bottom): AAP/REUTERS/Supri; p. 21: Alamy Stock Photo/Imaginechina Limited; pp. 22, 24: iStock.com/richardarno.

Every effort has been made to trace and acknowledge copyright. However, if any infringement has occurred, the publishers tender their apologies and invite the copyright holders to contact them.

NovaStar

Text © 2024 Cengage Learning Australia Pty Limited
Illustrations © 2024 Cengage Learning Australia Pty Limited

ISBN 978 0 17 033418 1

Cengage Learning Australia
Level 5, 80 Dorcas Street
Southbank VIC 3006 Australia
Phone: 1300 790 853
Email: aust.nelsonprimary@cengage.com

For learning solutions, visit **cengage.com.au**

Printed in Australia by Ligare Pty Limited
1 2 3 4 5 6 7 28 27 26 25 24

Nelson acknowledges the Traditional Owners and Custodians of the lands of all First Nations Peoples. We pay respect to Elders past and present, and extend that respect to all First Nations Peoples today.

Contents

Where Does Chocolate Come From?

Chocolate is one of the world's favourite treats. Chocolate, and foods and drinks with chocolate in them, is sold almost everywhere. But have you ever wondered where chocolate comes from, and how it is made?

Chocolate comes in many different kinds of foods.

A "Sometimes" Food

Although chocolate is a food, it's not an "everyday" food. Most chocolate is made with a lot of sugar and fat. This means it should only be eaten as a treat every now and then.

That's a Lot of Chocolate!

About 7.5 million **tonnes** of chocolate is eaten around the world every year.

A small car weighs about one tonne!

1 tonne of chocolate

a 1-tonne car

The most important ingredient in chocolate is made from the seeds of the cacao (say: *ka-kow*) tree. These seeds are called "cacao beans". Without cacao beans, there would be no chocolate!

However, turning cacao beans into chocolate bars is not easy. There are many steps along the way. Let's see how it is done.

cacao beans from a cacao tree

On the Cacao Farm

Chocolate-making starts with cacao beans, which are usually grown by farmers on cacao farms. Cacao beans come from the fruit of the cacao tree. Cacao fruit are called **pods**. Each pod is about the size of a rugby football and contains around 50 beans.

Growing Cacao Beans

Farming cacao beans takes a lot of time and effort. The trees can only grow in a warm and wet **climate**. Each tree needs a lot of water, and has to be protected from strong sun and wind. About five years after they are planted, cacao trees start to grow pods. After this, most trees grow pods twice a year.

a cacao farm

cacao pods

Two countries in Africa grow more than half the world's cacao – the Ivory Coast and Ghana.

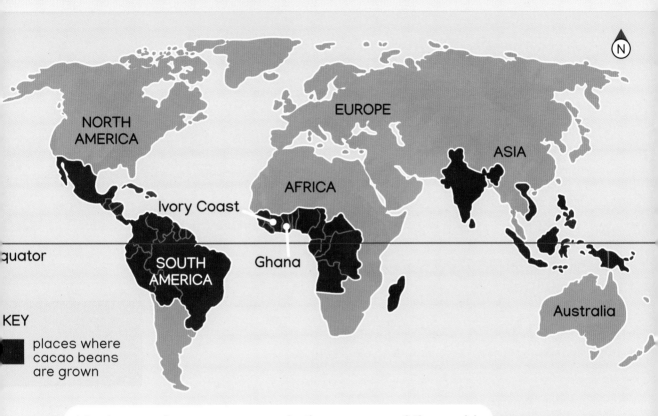

Most cacao beans are grown in these areas of the world.

Beans and Bars

Each cacao tree grows as many as 1200 cacao beans a year. This can make up to 1500 grams of chocolate, or 15 medium-sized chocolate bars.

Preparing Cacao Beans

When the pods are **ripe**, the farmers pick them and crack them open. They take out the beans and stack them in large piles or put them into boxes. Then they cover the beans with mats and leave them for about a week.

Ripe cacao pods are broken open to remove the beans.

While under the mats, the beans begin to go through some changes. By the end of the week, they have turned from a white colour to brown. They have also started to taste and smell more chocolatey.

Next, the farmers spread the beans onto trays in the sun to dry the beans out. They leave them there for about ten days. After this, the beans are packed into bags, ready to be sent to chocolate factories.

Cocoa beans are spread out to dry.

Cacao Farmers

There are about six million cacao farms around the world. Many of these are small farms run by families. Farming cacao is very hard work, and most farmers are paid very little money by the companies that buy their beans.

A farmer breaks open a cacao pod.

A Fair Price

Some chocolate **products** have labels that show that the cacao farmer was paid a fair price for their beans.

At the Chocolate Factory

Cacao beans are sent to chocolate factories all over the world. Most of these factories use special machines to do the chocolate-making work.

Making Cocoa

First, the beans are **roasted** in large ovens. After roasting, the beans are crushed in a machine. Their hard outer coverings are cleared away.

Cacao beans are scooped into a large oven for roasting.

What is left behind is the middle part of the bean. This is called the **nib**. The nib is the part that will be used to make chocolate.

cacao nibs

Next, the nibs are put into a **grinding** machine. This crushes the nibs and turns them into a paste. The paste is called "cocoa liquor" (say: *koh-koh lick-uh*). Cocoa liquor is then **separated** into brown cocoa **solids** and yellow cocoa butter.

Cacao beans are crushed up in a grinding machine.

Cacao or Cocoa? It's Confusing!

Once cacao has been roasted and crushed at the factory, it is known as "cocoa".

Making Chocolate

Chocolate is made from a mix of cocoa solids, cocoa butter and other ingredients, such as sugar and milk. However, turning these ingredients into chocolate is not simple. It can take many hours – or even days!

The first step is to put all the ingredients into a huge mixing machine. This machine has large steel or stone "grinders" that grind the mixture into a thick, smooth chocolate paste.

The ingredients are mixed into a smooth paste.

Next, the chocolate paste is put into another grinding machine that also slightly warms the paste. Doing this helps to improve the taste.

Finally, the chocolate is heated up again and then quickly cooled in a special cooling machine. This is called **tempering**. Tempering helps to harden the chocolate, so the chocolate does not melt easily.

Machines fill special trays with chocolate at a factory.

The chocolate is then formed into bars or other shapes. Finally, it is wrapped. Now, it's ready to be sold – and eaten!

Wrapped chocolate can be sold in shops.

Types of Chocolate

There are three types of chocolate: dark, milk and white. Each type is made up of a different mix of ingredients. Sometimes, ingredients such as fruit, nuts or caramel are added later.

dark chocolate

milk chocolate

white chocolate

Ingredients that Go into Chocolate

Dark Chocolate

cocoa solids

cocoa butter

sugar

Milk Chocolate

cocoa solids

cocoa butter

sugar

milk

White Chocolate

cocoa butter

sugar

milk

Chocolate Products

Different chocolate factories make different chocolate products. Some factories make bars and boxed chocolates to be sold in shops and supermarkets. Others sell the chocolate they make to chocolatiers. Chocolatiers are people who make very special chocolate creations. These include chocolates with fillings inside them and chocolate **sculptures**.

Chocolate comes in many shapes.

Chocolate sculptures can look like almost anything!

Some chocolate factories make other forms of chocolate, such as chocolate powder, liquid or paste. These are sold to food-making businesses to use in cakes, biscuits, sauces and drinks.

a chocolate drink

A bakery sells many different kinds of chocolate cakes.

Chocolate Everywhere

Chocolate is available almost everywhere. There are shelves of chocolate at the supermarket. We can buy it from corner stores, petrol stations or **vending machines**. Any shop that sells food will have some kind of chocolate product.

Chocolate-making is a worldwide business that is worth over 100 billion dollars. Australians spend nearly $200 each on chocolate every year. In the USA, each person spends about $145 a year on chocolate.

Many kinds of chocolate are sold in supermarkets.

Who Eats the Most?

The country where the most chocolate is eaten is Switzerland. Each person eats 170 grams per week (most chocolate bars are between 100 grams and 180 grams). That adds up to almost 9 kilograms of chocolate a year.

Chocolate might only take a few seconds to eat or drink, but it takes a very long time to grow and make. Next time you bite into a chocolate bar or sip a chocolatey drink, remember just how much work goes into turning a cacao bean into a special treat!

A Chocolatey Weekend

by Abby

Last weekend, I went with my mum to a chocolate sculpture **exhibition**. We also did a chocolate sculpting workshop. It was all amazing!

The first thing I saw when I arrived was a chocolatier at work. He was making a giant chocolate sculpture of a palace. It was taller than me!

As Mum and I walked around, we saw sculptures of birds and other animals that the chocolatiers had created. My favourites were two puppies. One was made from white chocolate and wore a green shirt. The other was made from milk chocolate and wore an orange shirt. They were so cute!

I decided I wanted to make a mouse at the chocolate sculpture workshop. One of the chocolatiers was there to help us. She showed me how to make the mouse's ears from white chocolate buttons!

In the end, I was really happy with what I made.

Mum says that my mouse looks too good to eat.

But I'm not sure!

Glossary

climate (*noun*)   the weather patterns throughout the year

exhibition (*noun*)   an event where objects such as artworks are arranged for people to look at

grinding (*verb*)   breaking into very small pieces

nib (*noun*)   the middle part of a cacao bean that chocolate is made from

pods (*noun*)   parts of plants that contain seeds

products (*noun*)   objects for sale

ripe (*adjective*)   ready to be picked

roasted (*verb*)   cooked in an oven

sculptures (*noun*)   handmade shapes

separated (*verb*)   split into parts

solids (*noun*)   things that keep their shape easily

tempering (*verb*)   quickly heating and cooling

tonnes (*noun*)   units of weight equal to 1000 kilograms

vending machines (*noun*)   machines from which people can choose and pay for items such as snacks

Index